The Christmas Standoff
at Moose Hollow

A Story that Crackles With Cranky Charm

By Patsy Stanley

Old ornery Ben Buckley had spent the past thirty Christmases alone in his little cabin up in Moose Hollow—a rangy, wind-whipped patch of high country where the grass grew tough around his cabin, the air stayed mean, and the varmints knew better than to go near his place.

Coyotes crossed the ridge line above his cabin at a respectful distance, raccoons held council meetings about avoiding Old Ben's property, and one particularly nervous porcupine was still in therapy after a run-in with Ben's snow shovel back in '02.

The raccoons had long since learned to steer clear, the crows refused to land on his roof, and even the bears gave his cabin a wide berth. He planned to keep it that way.

Varmints stayed away and neighbors didn't drop by unless they were lost, drunk, or both. Old Ben was a backwoods hermit who wore a coon skin cap and a huge scowl all the time. He liked it that way.

Old Ben was no fool-especially around Christmas time, when all those people in the village down below expected him to change and be some sort of sweetie pie! Ha!

The way Ben Buckley saw it, solitude wasn't a punishment—it was a hard-earned privilege. He'd done his time with people. Families gave him hives, church choirs sounded like dying geese, and every woman he ever met tried to get him to "open up." He did—right out the door. After all that, Ben came to one solid conclusion: most folks were more trouble than a wet fuse in a fireworks factory.

This Christmas, Ben had it all figured out: no fuss, no visitors, and hell no—no singing! Ben hated Christmas singing the way a cat hates bathwater. The sound of people harmonizing gave him indigestion. He'd rather listen to a chainsaw cut through frozen elk meat than a bunch of silly people belting out "Deck the Halls."

The last time somebody tried carol up close to his cabin, he'd let out a bark so fierce the coyotes packed up and left the county until New Years.

His holiday agenda was simple—one can of beans, a warm fire, and a splash of Grandpa's old "cough syrup," aged discreetly in the barn under a tarp labeled *Do Not Touch, Explosive Fertilizer.* He'd eat, burp, and grumble his way to Christmas morning. He'd drink enough to make him forget the lyrics to *Silent Night* and go to sleep without wishing anyone a merry anything.

Word got around the animal kingdom: *Ben Buckley don't like Christmas.*

But the thing about Christmas is, it's sometimes got its own sense of humor. Just when you think you're safe from it, it sneaks up the mountain on padded paws—usually dragging company you don't want...

Because this Christmas, something (or someone) was headed up the snowy road to Moose Hollow. And Ben

Buckley, against his better judgment, was about to find out what happens when an immovable grump meets an unstoppable dose of Christmas spirit.

Varmints. That's -what and who- it was. Who would have guessed? Not old Ben Buckley. Never...

The first varmint to show up was Toothless Jake, a half-blind raccoon from Ben's boyhood up on Moose Mountain. Jake waddled out of the tree line like he owned the place, dragging behind him a frozen chicken leg he'd found in a garbage can in the village below- and a stinky grudge that'd been fermenting since 1963—when young Ben had trapped Jake in a wood box. By the time the hefty little Jake gnawed himself out of the box, all his teeth were worn down to nubs. Been that way ever since.

The second varmint to show up was Gabby, a squirrel with attitude because of a limp she'd got the year Ben tried to invent "Squirrel Bowling" with a snow shovel and a frozen turnip that been a direct hit to her hip. Been limpin' ever since.

Gabby took one look at Ben's cabin and started chattering up a storm—cussing in squirrel language, which sounds like popcorn having a nervous breakdown.

The last varmint to show up was Old Gus, the hedgehog. Ben hadn't seen Old Gus since the infamous fire that left Old Gus with singed hair and a bald head.

The three of them-one raccoon with no teeth who foraged for leftover applesauce, marshmallows and oatmeal-ideal for the dentally challenged, one squirrel with a marked limp-who used to leap through the tree tops like lightning, one bald hedgehog with singed hair like a flattened scrubber pad —female hedgehogs had quite a laugh at that-which kept him mateless- stood swaying together outside Ben Buckley's cabin like a furry chain of mad Christmas rodents, ready to remind Ben Buckley of every dumb, mean, or half-cocked stunt he'd ever pulled on them. It was time to collect what was owed to them.

Ben squinted out the frosty window and saw the three varmints swaying in the snow, glaring at him.

He went to the cabin door and opened it a crack.

He said to old Gus. "Oh, for cryin' out loud, —you still holdin' a grudge about that fire? Who cares if you're bald?"

"And Jake-you got good eats down at that new restaurant in town."

Yeah, Gabby, you ain't shut up about it since I hit your hip."

"I don't know what you're here for, but forget it!-whatever it is!"

There was no earthly reason a squirrel, hedgehog and a raccoon from 1963 ought to be standing outside in a snowstorm wearing expressions that said, *We need to talk.*

"You ain't welcome here!" he barked.

Toothless Jake chittered, dragged the frozen chicken leg up the porch step like evidence, and jabbed a paw toward the other two. Gabby and Gus came closer, dragging a crate between them. Ben didn't like the look of it one bit. Crates usually meant trouble: tax audits, family reunions, or varmints with a plan.

He stepped out on the porch. Gonna' run 'em off! But they muscled the thing past him and inside before Ben Buckley could say boo. It was an old apple crate nailed shut and stamped in soot-black letters: **CHRISTMAS PAST – RETURNS.**

Ben followed them inside. Closed the door behind them.

"Aw, no you don't," Ben growled. "I sent all that back years ago."

The lid popped open anyway. Inside were the memories he'd hoped had died of frostbite long ago—like the year he'd booby-trapped the town's nativity scene with firecrackers.

Jake the raccoon dug through the box, holding up each memory like a prosecuting attorney while it played itself out, leaving Old Ben in a bad light each time. Gabby the squirrel did the talking. Gus the hedgehog belched for emphasis.

Ben took a swig from his jug. "You varmints done forgot somethin'. I don't do guilt, and I sure as hell don't do Christmas!"

Suddenly the wind outside howled loud enough to wake the dead—long, screeching words that sounded suspiciously like "Joy to the world, your bill has come due-" sung by a gang of other varmints Ben had encountered. Ben's kerosene lamp flickered and almost went out. The three varmints glared at him.

"Fine," he muttered. "If this is some kinda critter intervention, you best make it quick. I got beans burnin' and my patience expired two decades ago."

The wind heard him and howled harder, shaking the door like it wanted in. Ben squinted at the three.

"All right," he grumbled. "What's next? Y'all gonna show me how bad my life looks? I already know—it's sitting right here drinkin' midnight cheer on Christmas Eve with a raccoon, squirrel, and a bald hedgehog."

Old Gus growled low and motioned toward the frosted window. The glass shimmered, then cleared, like somebody had finally cleaned the past thirty years off of it. Ben looked through the window. Outside wasn't Moose Hollow anymore. It was Ben's old farmyard, the one he'd sold cheap because "neighbors kept happening."

And there he was—a younger, meaner, hairier Ben— chasing off a bunch of carolers with a snow shovel. The scene played like a bad TV rerun.

Gabby crossed her tiny arms. Jake pointed at the window and gave Ben a look that said, *Well?*

"Yeah, yeah," Ben muttered. "I didn't like that caterwauling. So what? That's history."

Jake the raccoon clacked his claws, and the view shifted again—to Ben last Christmas Eve, throwing a snowball at the church bell "for target practice." He'd missed the bell but nailed the mayor's car square on. The dent was still there, and rumor was, the mayor had been prayin' for a thunderbolt to take out Old Ben Buckley ever since.

Ben scowled. "That wasn't so bad."

Then the picture zoomed out to show a tiny stray dog nosing through Ben's trash that same night—looking for something to eat. Ben threw a boot at it. A steel-toed boot.

"Oh, for cryin' out loud," he said. "You varmints holdin' court now? That mutt stole my bacon!"

Old Gus growled again, long and low, like thunder warming up for judgment. The hedgehog stepped closer till Ben could smell his breath—earth, garlic, and something unholy from under the porch.

"All right, all right," Ben snapped. "Maybe I could've let the dog have the damn bacon!

The window darkened. The wind outside shifted tones—less howly, more whispery. The varmints backed off, and Ben's lamp brightened.

He sighed. "So that's it, huh? Why don't you three get out so I can keep mindin' my own business? Okay?"

Jake the raccoon tilted his head. Gus the hedgehog blinked. Gabby the squirrel started gnawing on the windowsill, which didn't seem like a good omen.

The air in the cabin went still. No crackle from the fire. No wind in the chimney. Just that thick, creepy quiet that says *something's about to happen and you're gonna' wish it didn't.*

The door opened, slow as guilty conscience. The three varmints ran out the door.

A snow filled wind rushed inside and propelled Old Ben out the door and onto the porch. Snow covered the world like an old bed sheet—lumpy, uneven, hiding things you'd rather never look at. The moon hung low over Moose Hollow, fat and full and cold and nosy.

Down in the hollow, Ben saw a wood cross sticking up out of a snow bank beside a rusted mailbox. On it was scrawled, in crooked letters:

Here Lies Mean Old Ben Buckley

Ben squinted. "Oh, for hell's sake."

From behind the snow bank came a sound—a shuffling, snuffling, growly little sound—and up popped Gus the hedgehog, now gray around the whiskers. Gus was dragging a tiny wreath.

Jake the raccoon and Gabby squirrel appeared next, both older, looking half spectral. Together, the three of them laid the wreath against the cross, stepped back solemn-like, and stared at Old Ben.

"Y'all think this is funny?" Ben barked. "That ain't my grave! I ain't even dead!"

Gus shrugged as if to say, *Not yet.*

Old Ben turned around to go back in his cabin. But the snow shifted again, stopping him, showing him a vision that made Ben's tough hide itch: his cabin, empty. The stove cold. The jug tipped over, long dried out. No varmints, no fire, no nothing—just silence, and the wind whistling through cracks that used to be his home.

Ben turned around and glared at the three varmints.

"That it? That's what happens? I freeze to death out here on the porch, and you three varmints use my bones for soup spoons?"

Toothless Jake nodded grimly. Gabby twitched her tail. Gus belched.

Ben stomped his boot. "Well, that's about the dumbest thing I ever heard! I ain't goin' out like that. I'm not dyin' till I'm good and ready—and when I do, it'll be because I picked a fight with something worth my time. Like a grizzly. Or a tax collector."

Ben stomped back inside and slammed the door shut. What a Christmas Eve!...

A short time later, something woke Ben up while he dozed in his recliner by the stove, his fire burning low, his jug half-empty. He scratched his beard.

"Well," he muttered, "guess that's what I get for mixin' moonshine with canned beans."

Something was off. He could feel it. He looked around. Not again! Three pairs of eyes were staring at him through the one window in his cabin.

Old Ben tried to ignore them, but three pairs of beady eyes can burn a hole clean through a man's hide. Finally, he stomped to the window and barked, "What do you want from me?"

A voice rang inside his head—clear as moonshine.

"Reparation!"

Ben blinked. "Repara—what? Speak English!"

The eyes didn't blink. He glared back.

Jake the raccoon opened his mouth wide and pointed a paw inside it.

"Ohhh," Ben groaned. "You want your *teeth* back?"

Gabby threw her paws out as wide as she could, wobbling dramatically.

"Uh-huh," Ben muttered. "You want a cape so you can fly again."

Finally, Gus the hedgehog ducked his head low, showing the bald patch right on top.

Ben snorted. "And you—you want me to knit you a wig so you can finally get yourself a girlfriend? Forget it!"

He turned back toward his chair, muttering, "You varmints got more demands than the tax office."

Suddenly, Ben's kerosene lamp went out in Ben's cabin. The wind began to howl. The door creaked and groaned. The floor pitched and heaved like it was tired of holding him up.

For the first time in years, **Ben Buckley was scared.**

"Well," he muttered, falling into his chair and gripping its arms, "mebbe' I oughta' give this a little more thought."

Instantly, the light blinked back on and the wind cut out—quiet as a guilty conscience. Ben blew out a shaky breath.

"Figures. You varmints got friends in the weather department."

He rubbed his chin, thinking. During the deep winters he liked to carve things—bowls, critters, spoons, anything to keep his hands busy and his temper in check. Maybe... maybe he *could* carve some teeth. He squinted toward the raccoon's reflection in the window. "Cedar, maybe pine."

He looked at the squirrel next. "And I got spare cloth. I sew my own britches. Guess I could stitch you a cape. Don't expect it to be fancy."

Then the hedgehog, who was rubbing his bald head like it owed him money. Ben sighed. "Now *you*... I'll have to think about. You're a tough case."

He made the strongest coffee he'd ever made, and drank a cup.

"Alright then. Let's see what I can do."

Old Ben dug through his junk drawers—spare buttons, twine, a busted harmonica, last year's fruitcake petrified into a brick—and found a block of cedar. He clamped it down, pulled out his pocketknife, and started carving.

A while later, Old Ben tossed the wood set of dentures out the door to Jake. Jake climbed back up to the window and stared in, grinning. The raccoon had himself a set of shiny cedar choppers. Jake grinned a huge smile.

Ben rummaged in the mending box, found an old pair of wool pants, and cut out a piece of the good leg. With a bit of twine and a needle, he sewed Gabby a cape—crooked, mismatched, but aerodynamic in theory. He threw it out the door to her. She tied it around her tiny shoulders, gave a jump, flew up to the cabin window and grinned in at Ben.

Ben figured he'd earned a quiet night after outfitting a raccoon with wood dentures and sewing a cape for a squirrel with no sense of direction. But no—there was the hedgehog to contend with.

A wig. What would he make it out of?

There came a faint scratching at the door. Ben knew it was the hedgehog, waiting.

Ben opened the door just a crack and peered out at Gus the hedgehog. His quills stuck out in every direction, frizzed and fried, giving him the look of a walking Brillo pad that had seen too many dirty skillets. Gus huffed through his nose, making a whistling sound like a teapot with opinions. Ben had singed the little guy years ago during an experiment involving fireworks and a coffee can.

Now here Gus was, still smoldering in spirit if not in flesh. Ben sighed, shut the door, and shuffled over to the food shelf, He grabbed a tin of bacon grease he'd been saving for emergencies—real ones, like squeaky hinges or dry biscuits. He took it to the door, opened it and threw the can out at Gus.

"There. Groom yourself. Try not to set anything on fire."

Gus stared, sniffed the can, then started smearing bacon grease across his quills with the confidence of a man at a barber shop who knows he's finally getting done right. In no time, he was slick, shiny, and smelled like breakfast.

Ben watched him. Gus still stared at him. There was more. Ben wrinkled his nose. "What?"

Gus snuffled and stared at Old Ben.

"You want something more. Figures."

He shut the door and looked around.

He grabbed this and that and tossed each one out the door to Gus. Gus nosed them all aside until Ben tossed out a ball of coal black tattered yarn he'd been saving since 1946. Gus grabbed it and popped it on his head. Then Gus ran to the window, climbed up to it, and swayed alongside the other two varmints.

Ben looked out at the three of them clinging to his only window. The raccoon grinned at him through his cedar teeth. The squirrel flapped her cape. The hedgehog kept grinning. He gleamed like a greasy bowling ball.

Old Ben shook his head and closed the inside storm shutters over the window. He'd had enough. He'd done his good deeds for the year. Maybe for the next decade. He shook his head and poured himself a cup of coffee.

"Next year," he muttered, "I'm puttin' up a *No Vacancy* sign."